That Job
Just Isn't Into You!

By Rob Harper

ISBN: 1463522703
ISBN-13: 9781463522704
LCCN: 2011908825
CreateSpace, North Charleston, SC

This book is dedicated to every worker who gets up everyday/or night and perform the act known as work.

∾

"Each of us has the right and the responsibility to assess the roads which lie ahead, and those over which we have traveled, and if the future road looms ominous or unpromising, and the roads back uninviting, then we need to gather our resolve and, carrying only the necessary baggage, step off that road into another direction."

Wouldn't Take Nothing For My Journey Now
by Maya Angelou

Contents

Preface

"You're fired! Did you hear me? You're fired! Get out! Don't even worry about cleaning out your desk. Just leave. Get the hell out!"

No. You're not on Donald Trump's *The Apprentice*. You're not having a nightmare either. The message might not have been delivered as severely as the one you just read, but it has become your reality. That cushy job you had a love–hate relationship with, the job that caused you to curse under your breath with regularity? That job is *over*!

Unfortunately, you are not alone. By the time you finish reading this, thousands of people around the world will share your fate and think the same thing you are thinking: "How the hell did I manage to mess it up? I need my job! Why me?" Before you start beating yourself up, allow me to say - it wasn't your fault. *That Job Just Isn't Into You!*

What?

No one sets out to be fired or laid off from a job, especially given the economy we live in, but it happens to the best of us. You know the old saying, "shit happens!" You don't like it. It makes you mad. No, it pisses you off, and it feels like the end of *your* world, but losing your job isn't the end of *the* world. Come on, breathe.

Sure, there's the initial sting. Everyone who loses a job feels it, but moving on from a job that wasn't for you can be the best thing for you and your career. Far too many people get stuck in dead-end jobs and want to leave but are afraid. Losing the job that had become your comfort blanket (similarly to Linus's blue blanket in *Charlie Brown*) could be just the push you need to get a better job and start a brighter future—if you let it. Turn the negative into a positive. Losing that job can get you out of a rut and open you up to self-discovery and new opportunities.

Stuck In a Rut

I have got to get free.
I can no longer fool myself into thinking that this is for me.
I must go out there and find what's out there for me.
I know that it is there. I only have to find it.
I know what it is.
I only have to do it.
Even if I don't succeed, at least I will know that I gave it a shot, a shot for me.
I will do my best. I will keep trying until I succeed or an avenue opens for me.
But remaining complacent—doing the same old thing—isn't stimulating or fulfilling.
I refuse to stand idly by and let the world pass me by.
I cannot and will not miss any more opportunities while others achieve.
I want to live my dream, be my dream, and create new dreams.
I will leave this dark, horrid abyss. I will go out there and do what I have to do.
I will strive. I will rise up high out of my rut and into creativity.
It's going to be a brand-new day.

೧൭

After reading the first few pages, you're probably thinking, "another self-help book that reads as though it's making fun of a serious matter in your life." Wait a minute. Before you get yourself all worked up, please understand one of my reasons for writing this book is to help you view the loss of your job in a different way. I want to share my story and the stories of others who have lost their jobs. Like you, we too, on more than one occasion, have experienced the loss of a job. In some ways, we have felt exactly the way you feel now—angry and depressed. It was hard for us to come to terms with the fact that a job we had slaved over just wasn't into us. Or we were at a job where we weren't satisfied and our careers had become stagnant. Like anyone else in our situation, we could have played the blame game and thrown ourselves a pity party. However, we realized we would only be hindering ourselves by not first accepting the job loss and then turning it into something positive. We took a leap of faith, reinvented ourselves, and found other jobs. Initially, our quest wasn't easy, for we doubted ourselves and our abilities. Losing a job you are good at can cause serious damage to one's ego, but never give in or give up! There is hope.

By sharing these experiences, I also want to help you avoid self-destructive behavior that is often associated with job loss. The bridges you burn today can prevent you from crossing over to success in the future. So pay close attention to what to do and what not to do once your job breaks up with you. Hopefully, these experiences will help you see that losing your job isn't the worst thing that could happen; neither is it the end of the world. Once you realize that the job loss might be for the best, as I did, you can make a new path for yourself down a road you never thought to take.

∽

The Road Not Taken (1915)

Two roads diverged in a yellow wood,
And sorry I could not travel both
And be one traveler, long I stood
And looked down one as far as I could
To where it bent in the undergrowth.

Then took the other, as just as fair,
And having perhaps the better claim,
Because it was grassy and wanted wear;
Though as for that the passing there
Had worn them really about the same.

And both that morning equally lay
In leaves no step had trodden black.
Oh, I kept the first for another day!
Yet knowing how way leads on to way,
I doubted if I should ever come back.

I shall be telling this with a sigh
Somewhere ages and ages hence:
Two roads diverged in a wood, and I—
I took the one less traveled by,
And that has made all the difference.

by Robert Frost

re·la·tion·ship/ri'lāSHən,Ship

Noun
The way in which two or more concepts, objects, or people are connected, or the state of being connected.

∾

CHAPTER 1

Your Job Is a Relationship

Like a relationship with someone you care about, your job is a relationship. You set your sites on the job. You inquire about the job. The job is on your radar and it notices you. Each interview becomes part of your courtship. You score and get the job. You and the job get to know one another. You start nurturing the job. You figure out your likes and dislikes. The job has its ebbs and its flows. It's uncertain at times and makes you mad and cry. It defines you and provides you with a degree of security. Over time, the job becomes routine and you settle into it, as you would settle into a marriage or any other loving relationship.

And then one day, the job decides it just isn't into you. After all you and the job have gone through, it's over. You were both so comfortable. But out of the blue, you're called into an office or conference room and told, "It's over." Well, probably not in those exact words. The version you heard was probably more polished and corporate, but it had the same terse meaning.

But…but…but…Nope. No buts. It's over.

Imagine being in a romantic relationship for ten years. You put the best years of your life into that relationship, for better or for worse. It's a shock to be told by your significant other, "Sorry but it's over. I don't feel the way I used to about you."

WTF! Where did that come from? How did you miss it? You then realize that all the signs were there. You were bored; so was your mate. You were both on different pages. You were growing apart, but still you kept hoping it wouldn't end. Finally, one day without warning, reality hits you like a ton of bricks! You're forced to accept what you subconsciously knew was coming. It's over!

Losing a job is the same way. You see it coming, but you hope you're wrong. You and the job were moving in different directions and you couldn't stop it. Is it over? Should you ask for a second chance, or just accept it?

Let's face it—for better or worse, you invested a great deal of time into the job. You put in a great deal of unpaid overtime. You saved the company money and the most you ever took in return was a ream of paper. There is only one pen at your house belonging to the company. The others you brought back. How could the job let you go? Hey, you had even started adjusting to the once-a-year, 2 percent salary increase, without a bonus. Doesn't that count for something? Where is all this hostility coming from? Where is the justice? Where is the love?

Like some relationships, jobs don't last forever and you have to be prepared to move on when they're over. Certainly there are those who come back for more and plead to stay, but you have to know when it's really over.

☙

CHAPTER 2

It's Over! Have a Party!

How do you know it's really over? In an intimate relationship, when your partner moves out and takes up with someone else, you pretty much know it's over. In a marriage, you receive divorce papers. On a job, you receive the proverbial pink slip, or you're called into a conference room and told that you're being let go. If that didn't get your attention, maybe being escorted out the door by security and having your employee badge confiscated did. These are unsettling realities that many of us face at some point in our careers, but don't sweat it. Have a party! The initial fact of your job being over can be a shock to your system. And it's okay to feel bad for a while, but don't drown yourself in self-pity to the point that you can't function. If it's any consolation, you are not alone in what seems like the end of your world. Remember, there are others facing this fate, and when it happens you want to be able to think rationally and plot your next move. Once you realize the knock of inevitability is at your door and that it's not going away, accept it and have a Freedom Party!

I know that telling you to have a party to celebrate your being fired, let go, or downsized is easier said than done. After all, a number of emotions and feelings—from crying, meltdowns, bargaining, anger, embarrassment, and acts of revenge—are in play. Things can get rather dicey now. The way you handle your emotions and feelings can make or break your career.

~

Job loss: See it as the beginning of something new. A new you who will have doors opened to experience new opportunities. Embrace this time and explore interests you never pursued! Believe it or not, that free time you have now—without a job—might not ever come again until you retire (if you are so lucky).

~

CHAPTER 3

Cry If You Must, but Do It at Home!

Your partner of years tells you he/she just isn't into you. It hurts, and you want to do the "ugly cry," as the popular TV-show host Oprah Winfrey describes it. Cry a river of tears. You shed tears of hurt and disappointment because the relationship is over. You have feelings and want to show them, or maybe you're crying with the hope of receiving compassion and a second chance at the relationship. You think that maybe if you cry hard and long enough, you'll save the relationship.

Because your job is a relationship, you will want to cry when they tell you it's over. A tear or two may form in the corner of your eyes, but don't let that tear drop! Doggone it! With all your might, keep those tears from falling. If you must cry, let the tears drop and roll once you have left the workplace. Cry on the way home or at home. Heck! Cry a river once you've been served your walking papers, but never at the office. If you allow the first tear to drop and a second, followed by a third, next comes the heaving and deep breathing. What purpose does it serve? You will only hate yourself later for getting emotional. The tears aren't going to change your destiny.

Crying will make you uncomfortable as well as the person giving you the news that it's over (not that you care how they feel).

Besides, at one point or another you probably told a colleague you would never let them see you cry if you were terminated. Suck it up! Don't cry. Begin your road to recovery by maintaining your grace and dignity.

ᖆᎧ

CHAPTER 4

The Meltdown: Don't Do It!

One of the biggest mistakes you can make when you are laid off or fear you will be laid off (and eventually are) is to behave irrationally and have a meltdown. Meltdowns come in two classes: normal and psycho.

Normal meltdown: Word spreads that layoffs are imminent. Though not confirmed, all signs point to you. You know you will be on the chopping block.

Paranoia takes hold and you start making mistakes on the job that you wouldn't ordinarily make. You start coming to work late, and when you do come, you are dressed in all black. You have decided to go Goth and dare anyone to question your new style. You start viewing your colleagues as the enemy and distance yourself from them. Once the ax finally drops, you become bitter and spiteful. And for what? First off, if you suspect you are going to be laid off, why not use that time to start planning your next move? Be honest with yourself: somehow you got news that your number could be up, so don't let it take you by surprise.

Albeit small, use that window of opportunity to mentally prepare yourself. And if nothing else, take home all the stuff you have accumulated through the years at the office (teddy bears, golf balls, pictures, candy canisters, piggy banks, toasters, shoes, clothes, condoms, and whatever else made you feel at home). What you don't want to do is act out and burn a bridge you may want to cross again later. Remember, it's a small world when you're looking for a job, and you may need the old job as a reference or source of job referral.

Psycho meltdown: You enter psycho meltdown territory when you decide to tell off your boss for being a lousy manager or flip off your HR generalist for not having your back when you reported the louse. No, this isn't the time to go back to your desk and erase or trash client files. As tempting as it may be, don't delete your colleague's presentation, even if you did all the work and they got all the credit. Don't post sticky notes next to the water cooler in the employee lounge about who doesn't like whom, or why another employee wasn't chosen to be laid off instead of you. You should also forget about leaving personal drawings of anyone you don't like in the bathroom stalls. Save the graffiti for your journal. As for the one last e-mail you were going to send, about Jerry the file clerk who's been knocking boots with Emily, the prim and proper office secretary: skip it. Forget about sending anonymous letters to anyone at the office telling them they should have been fired and not you. They can easily figure out who sent them. Forget about creating Facebook pages attacking your colleagues and your boss. Making a YouTube video slamming your boss and colleagues? Get it out of your mind! And avoid Twitter. Once you post your rantings on YouTube or Twitter, they will become part of cyberspace forever. Many companies do Internet searches for this type of stuff, and you don't want your name or image linked to it. Besides, it's just silly. Accept your fate and the fact that *That Job Just Isn't Into You!* Channel your energies into something positive.

∽

CHAPTER 5

Please Let Me Stay: I Ain't Too Proud to Beg

When it's over, it's over. Don't beg to stay and become a psycho.

Bargaining to stay on a job after your number is up is not a good move. Similar to a relationship, when your mate says it's over, it's over. Begging to stay won't help. If you stay, you will get the short end of the stick in the long run. The same applies to a job. I know someone reading this will disagree, and there are a few books on the market advising just the opposite of what I suggest. However, I feel strongly against bargaining to stay on. I have spoken with many HR representatives, and they have said a great deal of planning is involved when a company decides to lay off an employee. Most companies (the good ones) do consider other options before making a final decision to reduce staff. The decision to let an employee go isn't made lightly and is often the last resort. Some employers will see if they can place the talent in other areas of the company. If not, companies will put together packages that will aid the soon-to-be-laid-off employee in their search for another job by providing them with severance pay and professional contacts.

But let's say you decided to negotiate remaining on your job (you have great bargaining skills). Even if you are successful and manage to strike a deal, it's only a matter of time before you're back on the chopping block. Something else to remember is the animosity you will develop toward your boss for putting you on the chopping block in the first place. Also consider that if you stay, it could mean a pay cut and more work. Do you really want that? No matter how you slice it, trying to bargain away the inevitable probably isn't in your best interest.

The time you think you bought by staying at your job is borrowed time, and it will turn into anger, for now you realize you are expendable and *That Job Just Isn't Into You!* If you're fortunate enough to remain on, you don't want to develop a bad reputation either. Staying at a job that doesn't want you could bring out the worst in you. As hurt as you might be, think about the years it took you to build a stellar reputation with the company. Creating drama after delaying the inevitable will diminish an otherwise untarnished reputation. Remember what I said earlier: you don't want to leave on a bad note. However, if you insist on going out with a bang, be prepared to be escorted out by security and to lose what little severance package the company might have offered you. Not to mention, you will place your name on the company's list of psycho employees. You will never be able to go back to that company for employment or use them as a reference. Is that what you want? Trust me: bow out with grace and plan a party. After all, being let go now makes you one of the lucky few who escaped, and probably with a nice severance package, if you played your cards right.

So accept your fate and run, don't walk, out the door to your freedom and endless opportunities.

∽

Take this job and shove it
I ain't workin' here no more
My woman done left and took all of the reasons
That I was workin' for.

You better not try to stand in my way
When I'm walkin' out the door
Take this job and shove it
I ain't workin' here no more

Well, I've been working in this factory
Pretty close to fifteen years
I've seen some of my best friends' women
Drownin' in a pool of tears

I've seen a lot of kinfolks dyin'
I had a lot of bills to pay
Lord, I'd give the shirt right off my back
If I had the guts to say, say what?

Take this job and shove it
I ain't workin' here no more
My woman's done left and took all of the reasons
That I was workin' for

The foreman is a regular S.O.B.
And the night boss, he's a fool
He got himself a brand new flattop haircut
Lord, he really thinks that's cool

One of these days I'm gonna blow my top
And that's shockin,' he's gonna pay it
Well I can't wait to see their faces
When I get the nerve to say, say what?

Take this job and shove it!

Written by David Allan Coe
Sung by Johnny Paycheck

CHAPTER 6

Anger: Don't Take It Personally

In the words of Sonny Corleone from *The Godfather*: "You are taking this very personally. Tom, this is business and this man is taking this very, very personally."

I'm angry as Hell! How dare they let me go! Stupid Jerks! Don't they know I need that job!

Feelings of anger after losing a job are normal. You are angry with yourself. Angry with your boss. Angry with your colleagues who weren't laid off. You're angry with everyone. *Why me?*

You did your best or tried doing your best. It just didn't work. What more could you have done? *Nothing!* You are human and not a robot. Don't take the job loss personally. Forget about revenge, which is not the best course of action (reread chapter four). Simply accept the fact *That Job Just Isn't Into You!*

☙

P. S. If you decide to go out with a bang (swearing, screaming, crying, and everything else), you probably should be embarrassed. This book might not be for you. Try reality TV.

CHAPTER 7

Embarrassment

There seems to be a stigma attached to losing a job. A person loses a job and is immediately ostracized. For what? Close colleagues of ten years or more become estranged. Even admitting to knowing the person who lost his or her job seems to be uncomfortable. Former colleagues avoid contact with the unfortunate person, going so far as to cross the street when they encounter each other in public. Some individuals will stop frequenting certain restaurants out of fear they might run into their former colleague. You would think the person had the bubonic plague. The only thing that's changed is his or her employment status. The person no longer works for the company. Don't be embarrassed after receiving your walking papers, nor should you be afraid to stay in contact with former colleagues.

I know companies make it seem as though you've done something wrong. They single you out by getting you to walk to the boss's office or conference room in the middle of the day to deliver the news *That Job Just Isn't Into You!* Your colleagues know what's about to happen and won't even look at you. After getting the news, it seems that everyone wants to avoid you like the plague. There isn't any air in the office until you leave. Man! Although it feels like one, it isn't a perp walk. You did nothing wrong. Hold your head up high. Leave the office with grace and pride. So what if you got canned? It happens to the best of us. *That Job Just Isn't Into You!* Either you didn't have the skills to keep the job, couldn't perform at the required level, had a personality clash with someone, were disliked by management, or the company was downsizing and your position was discontinued. Even if you had the skills to do your job, who's to say your boss wasn't threatened by you? If you were caught stealing, you definitely weren't the right person for the job. But, hopefully, you didn't lose your job because of sticky fingers or a toilet bowl tongue.

Look at it this way: unemployment today is reaching epic proportions. With your job loss, you join the ranks of an exclusive club of individuals (ranging from CEOs to short order cooks). Consider yourself fortunate. Many people will share this status at some point in their lives.

ᕙᕗ

CHAPTER 8

Acceptance of the Pink Slip

No more anger and embarrassment

Downsized. Discontinued. Displaced. Forced to resign. Pick one; it happened to you. Accept it. Of course you don't want the pink slip, but what else can you do? Tear it up in your boss's face? Not a good move. Remember, you don't want to leave on a bad note. The way I see it, with pink slip in hand and permanently etched in your memory, you can do a couple of things: accept it or drown yourself in pity. The latter choice is dangerous. Let's walk through the first option.

You receive your pink slip. Cry for a day. Stay in bed for a day. Get mad and then angry. After a few days pass, you're in survival mode. You can focus on your next steps. Securing a job and not creating any unnecessary expenses are your main concerns now. Either you will go after that dream job, or take a job (any job) until the next best thing comes along.

Second option: you go to the nearest watering hole to clear your head and let off steam. You order your first drink and then a second. Then you start ordering drinks for anyone who will listen to your pitiful story about how your asshole of a boss should have been fired instead. Later you stumble home, sleep, and wake up the next day around noon with a hangover. You have your cup of coffee, then you realize you were fired. You're angry, but become enraged when you see the receipt from the tab you ran up at the watering hole the night before. The tab you ran up will probably incense you more than the fact that you were fired. You created another expense that you don't need.

I recommend accepting the fact *That Job Just Isn't Into You!* Have your freedom party or just reflect on what you had, and then plan your next move.

 ∾

CHAPTER 9

Guilt after Being Set Free

Carpe diem!

Eventually, the reality of losing your job starts to settle in. Although you're not completely over the job loss, you've started to move on. You sleep in almost every day. Why not? You stayed up late the night before munching and watching David Letterman, Jimmy Kimmel, and Jimmy Fallon. On the days you do get up early, you walk or drive around—depending on what's practical in your geographical location—people watching. You are amazed at what you see. People are getting up and going to work. Some are smiling. Some are frowning and others clearly need that fresh cup of Starbucks coffee to help them get started. Some evenings you meet up with buddies or girlfriends for drinks. You listen to their work (war) stories, all the while thinking *that used to be me*. Some of their stories are funny and some depressing. Story after story. The typical work drama. One person hates the job, but it's a job. Another person knows layoffs are on the horizon and isn't sure who will be let go. There's always someone in the group who wishes he/she were laid off so that they can do something else. Before long you want to share a work story, but you don't have a job. You feel guilty. Should you have had that freedom party after all? You wonder how you came to lose your job? Damn it! That used to be you. Getting up and rushing off to work. At times you weren't sure if you were happy or sad, but you had a job. What's wrong with this picture? *Stop!* Don't look back. It's not your fault your job is over. Remember, *That Job Just Isn't Into You!*, and, truth be told, you weren't into the job. Stop feeling guilty. There are better things out there for you.

৩৯

Today's job market isn't the market our parents or grandparents worked in. Companies are no longer faithful to you, so why should you be faithful to them by sticking around when you're unhappy? Bet you never thought about it that way.

Start asking friends about potential jobs. Work your contact list. Don't become a recluse, and don't be afraid to make it known that you lost your job.

৩৯

CHAPTER 10

Depression

Who wants me?

For some people breakups are not a big deal. They breakup with one person, and before the day is over they are with someone new. For others it isn't quite as easy, especially if they felt blindsided by the breakup. The same can be applied to a job search. Some people lose a job at the beginning of the week, and before the week is over they have another job. Others aren't so lucky. Before finding something new, they become depressed.

You are on the road to discovery and recovery. You accepted the job loss. The anger, embarrassment, and guilt are gone. You have sent out résumés and you're going on interviews. You are empowered! You feel as though you can stand in the middle of the street and say, *Yeah, I'm a winner!* The outlook is promising. You're on the road to recovery. Who needs that old job? You'll show them what you're made of. They will hate that they let you go. Your mojo is back. Any moment you will be back in the workforce, bigger and better than ever. You're just waiting for it to happen now.

Why isn't the phone ringing? The interviewer said you were good. You were the top candidate. No one is calling for a follow-up interview. What's happening? Vulnerability besieges you. Was there a better candidate interviewing for the same job? Did you answer a question wrong? Did you wear the wrong suit? Was there something in your teeth? Who wants you? Who is going to hire you? Do you have what it takes? Like that old relationship, you don't know anything else but the old job. How long before something new comes along?

Don't give up!

Stay focused. That dry spell and those feelings of inadequacy are normal. One moment you're going on interviews and the next: nothing. Don't despair. Take a deep breath. Reread the quote at the beginning of the book by Maya Angelou and the poem by Robert Frost. There is a slight possibility you are on the wrong road. You could be on a path you shouldn't be on. In other words, is the job you are trying to get really for you? Are you looking for another job that won't be into you?

∽

Always look for the next best opportunity. Don't settle for what you have. You never know when the current job will be over. Unlike personal relationships, where you want to be satisfied with one person (at least most of us do), it's okay to cheat and fantasize about the next big job, providing you do more than fantasize...you have to act on it!

∽

CHAPTER 11

Rediscover Yourself

The job you once allowed to define you is gone. You're gone. Are you really gone? You didn't realize it at the time, but you became so wrapped up in the job that you started to define yourself by the job. Similarly, many people define themselves only in the context of their love relationship—both are fallacies that create enormous problems when jobs or loved ones are lost. Rediscovering yourself is the only way out. The same way a person identifies him or herself with his or her mate, your entire life became the job, and it made you miserable. You allowed yourself to become obsessed with the job, even when the job started losing interest in you. It wasn't as obsessed with you as you were with it. That's why it decided to let you go. Now that it's over, rediscover who you really are. Reconnect with the real you. Now that the old job is gone, baby, reinvent yourself with a new attitude. The first step is rediscovering your passion. What is it you would like to do? Do you want to go back to school, teach, dance, act, become a chef, a realtor, or even host your own reality TV show? It's all yours for the taking. Rethink the hobby you love so dearly and turn it into a job.

More often than not we deny ourselves what we really want and end up settling. You really didn't want to be in the relationship with your significant other. You felt it had run its course, but you were afraid to leave because it was all you knew. When you began your search for something new, you looked for the same type of relationship. The same thing can be said of the dead-end job search. You are looking for the same type of job. You are free now; explore other opportunities. The job didn't want you then, and it probably won't want you now. It's time to rediscover.

There is a large percentage of people who hate their jobs. Most of them took the job as a means to an end, as opposed to taking the job and using it as a stepping-stone to other opportunities. They remained in the job out of fear of looking for something else. Never settle for that dead-end job; it won't be faithful to you and will eventually discard you. Remember, *That Job Just Isn't Into You!*

There is only one way to look at a job. See the job for what it really is—a job. It is not you. Don't allow a job to define you as a person. If you do, once the job is done with you, it will discard you, and you will find yourself lost. You are better than the job and you will get a better job.

Stories from the Battlefield

∾

CHAPTER 12

Advice from a Pro

June Weinstein
President/Owner of Walsh Associates

"You have to be persistent," says June Weinstein, the owner of Walsh Associates, a job placement agency that specializes in providing financial operations and support personnel to the banking and brokerage communities in New York City and nationally. "You should select a handful of agencies, two or three that specialize in your field, and send your résumé." She also suggests posting your résumé on Monster or join LinkedIn. "Those are really good sites to post your résumé," she confirms. Talking to former colleagues is another good resource when looking for jobs.

Mrs. Weinstein, who has been in the job placement business for a number of years, is recognized in the industry as a go-getter, having built her agency after working as a salesperson making five dollars an hour. "I was determined to make it when I entered the work force. I was divorced, had a son, and a teacher's degree. I started working as a sales rep. I would get to work early and go up and down the floors of my building, selling ads from top to bottom."

Her persistence and determination eventually paid off and in a few years allowed Mrs. Weinstein to purchase and grow the current agency she has now. "When it seems that what you are doing isn't working, change careers and reinvent yourself, but never quit." She also said that she wouldn't recommend relocating for a job. "I know some people would disagree with me, but I wouldn't chase a job. You are going to a new area and once you get there and you don't like it, you have to come back (if you can)." She suggested staying where you are while continuing to search. "You will eventually find what you are looking for, even if you have to start your own business."

⁘

Persistence
Nothing in the world can take the place of persistence.
Talent will not;
Nothing is more common than unsuccessful men with talent.
Genius will not;
Unrewarded genius is almost a proverb.
Education will not;
The world is full of educated derelicts.
Persistence and determination alone are omnipotent.

—Calvin Coolidge

CHAPTER 13

You Mean You're Dumping Me On Our Anniversary?

My Story

I used to think only incompetent people lost jobs. If you weren't incompetent, you had to be a bad person, though I'm not sure how I defined "bad person." This was my thinking until I joined the ranks of people who have been laid off. And I know I wasn't incompetent or a bad person. My job was no longer into me and it let me go. When I was laid off, it was a bittersweet experience. Bitter in that I was leaving behind a great staff of people who supported me tirelessly; and sweet in that I was free from a job that wasn't for me.

When I was laid off from my banking job at Citi Private Bank in 2008, I called my staff once I left the building. I wanted to break the ice and let them know I was okay with being laid off and that they shouldn't worry about me. I also told them they should continue doing a great job. I wanted to avoid that awkward feeling of meeting on the streets or in a store without talking first.

I was laid off from my job after nearly fifteen years of service. Having worked my way up from a contractor to a vice president, you would have thought my job was secure and that I would retire with the company. However, during those fifteen years, many times I told myself, *leave—this isn't for you.* But for some strange reason, I stayed. Looking back on those years, I can't say why I stayed. Maybe I enjoyed the company of my colleagues. Some were delightful to work with and others were self-absorbed individuals—just there for the ride, or so it seemed. While I did meet my closest friends (friends to this day) at the job, some of them left the company before I did. I can't even say it was for the money. Maybe I stayed for the bragging rights of working for a major Fortune 500 company in the financial industry. Or maybe I fell into thinking, self-importantly, that "the job really needs me." You know the feeling: nothing can happen without you being there, for the job ceases to exist without you. The job needs me and you! Even if we hate the job more than we like it. We are there on time and feel guilty if we are a half-second late. We make things happen on the job on a daily basis that wouldn't ordinarily happen. *The job really needs me.*

I certainly felt that way, until I was laid off on my fifteenth anniversary. Ouch! A slight sting, but when my number was up, it was up. Reality check. I didn't freak out. As a matter of fact, because I had so much going on with my personal life, I welcomed the opportunity for something new when I discovered that the job just wasn't into me. You read it right. I saw the layoff as an opportunity, and I welcomed it. To be honest, it was an opportunity I should have taken years earlier, but I waited fifteen years for the job to say it just wasn't into me.

Months before I exited stage left, I felt the end was near. I just didn't know how near. In the weeks leading up to my freedom, I mentally began to prepare myself. I had cleared my office and had taken home all my personal belongings. To be honest, there wasn't much for me to clean up and take home. Unlike most people who build a shrine to themselves in their office or at their desk, I only had a picture of my dog (Sir Lancelot of Jonesboro, aka Lance) and a bottle of tap water. Yeah, I know the talk about how we spend most of our lives at work, so we want to make it feel like home. Perhaps, but I believe that when it's time to go, be ready to go without delay. If you recall, the financial community began hemorrhaging in 2008. Rumors were rampant that Citi would be slashing its workforce. I was part of the management team; management doesn't bring in revenue. We were considered a cost center. Usually, these areas are hit first with layoffs. Anyway, because my staff started getting restless over the layoff rumors, I went to my manager and asked if there were to be layoffs in our department (which had a few months earlier been consolidated with another cost center). My manager responded that no one would be laid off. All the while, people were being ushered in and out of meetings with HR and were seen coming out in tears and looks of disbelief. Huh?

By January 2008, it was evident that my department would be affected by layoffs. Can you guess who the lucky guy was? Me! You should have seen the look on my face. That moment is forever etched in my memory. I was sitting in my office (remember, nothing personal was there) looking through employee manuals. My manager asked me to join him in a meeting. I got up from my desk. With my chest a tad bit poked out, I followed him into a conference room. Inside the room, sitting behind a table, was our department's HR rep. On the table were water, napkins, and cups. I took my seat on the opposite side of the HR rep. My manager sat at the head of the table and started to nervously read what I call the breakup letter. It was actually a standard separation agreement that companies are required to read. The HR rep seemed a bit nervous also. I don't know why. I was the person being set free, and I wasn't going to go postal. My record with the company was exemplary. After the breakup letter was read, I was offered water. I declined and suggested they have a drink. All the years I had given the company: my devotion, my expertise, my presence, my commitment, and my time. In a matter of minutes it was over. I was offered another job with the company and was told to take some time to consider it, but I knew what my answer would be. I had done my time with the company. The sound of inevitability was at my door, and I accepted it. But in the spirit of things and not to appear mad or angry, I agreed to consider the offer. After my HR rep read me my final job rites, she asked if I needed to go back and clean my office. I smiled and said it wouldn't be necessary. I only needed to get my coat. She seemed a bit surprised at my answer. And just like that, my fifteen years with the company had come to an end.

I tried to contain the excitement growing inside me until I left the building. Before I could get on the elevator that would lead me to my freedom, my boss stopped me in the elevator bank to shake my hand and bid me farewell. As if he really cared that I was leaving. He was probably thinking *better him than me*. Had the roles been reversed I might have thought the same thing. I shook his hand and stepped onto the elevator. I didn't even give him the bird going down to the lobby. Once outside the building, I felt as though a load had been removed from my shoulders. Interestingly enough, I ran into a dear friend who had worked at the same company years earlier and told her what had happened. She smiled and said, "It's about time. Good for you. Now go do what you're supposed to do." Interesting that she would say that, I thought. As I walked away from my old job, I called members of my staff and told them what had happened and wished them the best of luck.

I then went home and did a postmortem of my career. I looked at where I had been, what I had done, and where I wanted to go. Being a writer by trade, I knew I wanted to write, so I started blogging and sharing my story about being laid off. Two of the stories were published on CNN iReport. One was titled, "That Job Just Isn't Into You" (this book's namesake) and the other, "It's Over! Have A Party!" I refused to look back at my old job. At the moment, writing was where my heart was. That's were I wanted to be. Not only was 2008 a taxing year for me professionally, but I was also dealing with the decline of my sister, whose seven-year battle with lung cancer was gradually coming to an end. Writing became cathartic for me. I had no time to be sad or angry over my job loss.

While writing about job loss and politics (the 2008 election was in full swing), another job opportunity presented itself with another financial institution. Having just been let go from the world of finance after fifteen years, I wasn't exactly in a rush to go back. With my savings, a generous severance package, and my freedom to write, what more could I have asked for? Not only that, but what more would I possibly want to do? When I left the world of finance, I was chief of staff of my department. I really didn't want that big of a responsibility again. My headhunter, however, suggested that I at least go in for an interview. I interviewed for the job and ended up accepting the position, as it was for a short term. While the work environment for this position wasn't exactly the best, the job did allow me flexibility to travel and be with my sister. The job lasted all of two years. The stories I could tell you about those two years would make your head spin, but I'll save them for a different book. There were suggestions of being hired full time, however, for me, when it was over, it was over. You have to know when to move on and not look back.

I am always considering new relationships in my career. I enjoy flirting with the endless possibilities of opportunities. I am not sure which one I will choose or if I will choose and entertain any seriously. They are all attractive, enticing and with certain benefits. I will take my time and decide which one is best for me. I will then choose, but always being aware that if it doesn't fit, I will move on for there is that reality that job just isn't into me. The possibilities can be endless.

∽

CHAPTER 14

The Bills Don't Stop Once the Job Ends

Debbie's Story
Administrative Assistant for International Association of Machinists &
Aerospace Workers, District 143

I was resigned to the fact that I was being laid off from my job because I knew it was coming. I was given two weeks' notice, but knew way ahead of my notice that I would be laid off because of bargaining failures with the airline labor union I worked for. I did get upset the week after I was laid off. I loved my job, and it was hard to come to grips with it being gone for good. Actually, my entire office closed, so about five people were affected. We were a close-knit group and had worked together for some time. It felt weird not having to go into work. Getting up in the morning and heading off to my job was my routine. It was a part of me and then it was gone.

Once my job ended, my immediate concerns were my finances. The job might have ended, but the bills didn't. They kept coming. Knowing I was getting a severance package gave me some relief.

Less stress. Also having a husband with a job wasn't bad either. The severance package was nice, but I don't know if it would be considered generous, as I have never received one before. I'd never been laid off before.

I am currently looking for work, and I do not want to settle for any job. I want to do something I enjoy. There are jobs out there, but there are so many people looking for work that it has been hard getting an interview. Despite all my experience with an airline union, I have yet to get called in for an interview. I've thought about going back to school for a trade or something. At this point, I haven't taken any steps to do that, but it's still an option. Right now my husband tells me to relax, which I will try to do. I have much more time to spend with my family, and I definitely enjoy that. I also noticed I am pretty good at this whole housewife thing. So until something else comes along, I think I will take my husband up on his offer.

൶

CHAPTER 15

There's a Lot of Fish in the Sea of Jobs

Douglas's Story
Mortgage Banker/Underwriter/Former Consultant for IBM

People approach their job in different ways. Some want the job for life. Others just want the job for a paycheck and without commitment. In today's work environment, most jobs last for five or six years. If you are there any longer, you have to ask yourself what you are doing (especially if you are in the same position and not happy). If you aren't happy, recognize it (the job) is not for you and not right. Those are signs to start doing something, while you still have a choice. I realized my job wasn't working before the job told me. The job just wasn't into me, and I wasn't into the job.

When I was laid off from my job with IBM, I got the news from a phone call that was no different from a telemarketing call. After being with the company for a little over four years, I recognized IBM (the area I worked in) was dysfunctional. I was a contractor for IBM hired to do different assignments as they came up. I didn't like it, but I was equipped to deal with it. I had gone on a few assignments before things started drying up. I waited for eight months, or sat on the bench as they call it. I didn't know what was happening, though I was still getting paid. Somehow I knew the ax was going to fall. Finally, when the phone call came I was not shocked. I was surprised it hadn't come sooner. Initially, I thought my performance review rating of a three had something to do with my being let go. Rating level three is considered average and middle-of-the-road. Companies usually rate employees as level threes when they are looking to make layoffs. Anything less than a three is considered good and anything greater is considered bad. I talked to my colleagues about the rating, and each had received a level three rating. We thought it was bullshit! There was no possible way we were all performing at the same level. I mean, come on. Someone had to be performing above average or below. Anyway, it became evident to me that my time with IBM was coming to an end, and this job probably wasn't supposed to be for me.

After I was let go, I got a severance package. It was okay. The economy was going bad when I got laid off, but I wasn't apprehensive. I drew a line in the sand. I set up a timeline for myself. I expanded where I was going to search for work. That meant looking in different fields outside my comfort zone. Some people only look at one field and one geographical area. You must be willing to relocate for work, if required. There is a trade-off if you want to stay in the same geographical area and the job market is dry. Unless you are an entrepreneur, be willing to move. You must condition yourself to the labor market you are in. Within thirty days, I had another job. The way I see it, looking for a job is like going fishing. Throw your line in the water and see who's biting and who isn't. I reached out to contacts in my Rolodex and put the word out that I was looking for a job. Because I was known for my strong work ethic, my contacts contacted people they knew and gave me recommendations for jobs. At the request of my friends, I then sent résumés to their contacts. Initially, I got nervous when I didn't receive any responses, but I didn't allow myself to panic. We become creatures of habit. When we no longer have what we expect from our daily lives, we panic. To make certain I didn't feed into my nerves, I went on vacation instead of waiting by the phone. At the end of thirty days, I was offered another job with better pay and a better working environment.

In everyone's job there are signs that things are not right. You can choose to deal with them or leave for a better job. Always listen with a third ear when you are feeling uncomfortable about your standing at a job, and have a backup plan.

౿

CHAPTER 16

It's Easy to Find a Job While You Have a Job

Laura's Story
Former quality assurance manager at ComputerShare/Consultant

I didn't know it was going to happen, but getting laid off was a relief for me. There was too much stress. I didn't like it at all. I was only at the bank for three years. Prior to that, I was a manager at ComputerShare, a computer software solutions and professional service company. Twenty-nine years I was there, and one day they told us the company was being bought out by an Australian company and we wouldn't have jobs. All of our jobs were being transferred to either Australia or Canada. I guess they felt we were making too much money, so we were let go. You feel bad. It hurts—you feel so unnecessary. You feel like you're a piece of crap. You work for a company for so long, and then it's up. Why let people go who have experience only to hire someone else to do the same job without experience? But what can you do? You can't do anything about it.

When I learned that we would be laid off, I started looking. It's always easier to find a job when you have a job. I don't think people realize they should look at the postings in their company to see if there are other jobs available. I started looking online at job postings and talked to people that I knew. I got an interview with Bank of New York Mellon, and they hired me. They paid me 20 percent more then I had been making at ComputerShare. When I was laid off a second time, it was kind of a relief. Now, I would have preferred to be working, but I took advantage of the time I had off and did things that I hadn't been able to do. I spent a lot of time with my family. I golfed with my sister, went walking, and I cooked a lot. I enjoy cooking.

The job I have now is consulting. If this job ends, I will look for another job. I've always wanted to go back to school. I might do that. One good thing is that I have always saved my money, so if I need to fall back on something, I have some savings. I've told my kids the same thing. Put money aside in case you need it.

You should always make it a habit to put aside money when you're working. Don't spend all your money. You always need a cushion to fall back on, just in case your job plays out. If your job does end, always have a backup plan.

◦◦

CHAPTER 17

Always Have a Side Gig

Nelson's Story
Investment Broker/Corporate Consultant/Salsa Instructor

I've been laid off twice. Each time there was a year between jobs. You do feel bad after you are laid off. I went into a depression. Not clinically, but there were days I would stay in bed all day. Wake up and okay, you lost that day, but it gets better. You have to stay busy because you have time on your hands until you get another job. I would do things I hadn't done before. I would to go museums, the Statue of Liberty, and run errands for people. I also did volunteer work. Not in the sense of real volunteer work, but I would volunteer to give people rides to the store or lay sheet rock—miscellaneous things to stay busy.

You don't give up. Find your passion, something you do well. Play music well? Can you teach? Find what you are good at and do it. I am from a military family, and I had wanted to join the military during the Gulf War, Operation Desert Storm. An uncle who had been in Vietnam talked me out of it, but that was my passion. I now enjoy writing, running, and dancing. I fell back on dancing when I was laid off for the second time in my financial career. The second job loss was a blessing in disguise because my father became ill, and during the time I had off, I was able to take care of him. I also started teaching salsa and boxing classes. It helped pay the bills, and I didn't have to dip into my savings. Plus, I was doing something that I loved.

Because you don't know what will happen with a job, my advice is to follow your passion and always make certain you can do a variety of different things. The days of staying in the job for the gold watch are pretty much gone. You have to be ready to change. Every day is different. What matters is what you can do going forward. You just have to keep going.

Right now, I am learning to play the flute and my girlfriend is teaching me German.

$\backsim$

CHAPTER 18

Step Out of Your Comfort Zone

Yvonne's Story
Nurse Manager of ED (Emergency Department) at Veteran's Hospital
Associate Director of Nursing (ADON)

I liked my old job. I was there for twenty years. I liked what I did as the associate director of nursing, but there were drawbacks. I was a manager, but I didn't see any growth, and I was away from home and my two sons a great deal.

I did some soul-searching and decided to either step out on faith and the belief that I could do better and get another job or stay in the current position for the next twenty years. Naturally, there was no guarantee that if I stayed with the old job it wouldn't eventually disappear. I decided to take a chance.

I was always milling it around, trying to put on paper what I wanted to do next. I guess I stayed as long as I did out of fear. I was both frightened and comfortable in my position. I could do the job easily. I am a single parent of two teenage boys and was comfortable. I had security, health insurance, a paycheck, and I didn't want to gamble away something I'd had for twenty years. I kept thinking to myself, if I leave my current job as ADON and didn't like the new one, I wouldn't be able to go back. I also remembered when I got my job as ADON, I had also interviewed earlier for my dream job as a flight nurse. The flight nurse job, I wanted. I would have been the head nurse responsible for caring for patients being flown from one hospital to another. Unfortunately, I didn't get the dream job and I was glad, because a month later I became ill. And had I gotten the flight nurse job, I would have to have waited before my health insurance kicked in. That experience scared me. I was glad it didn't work out. I stayed with the old job, but still wanted something more. Then I started thinking about the economy not being good and wondered what would happen if I couldn't get another position. I thought of everything. Finally, I said to myself, just look at the people who have been at jobs for thirty plus years and then lose their jobs. I also thought about people at jobs that they shouldn't be at, but were there because, like me, they were afraid to leave and try something new. I thought, *what do I have to lose?* and I started sending out résumés. When I didn't get callbacks from the initial set of applications, my self-doubt started to creep back. I knew that I knew my stuff. I saw others being hired around me for other jobs. I knew I was qualified. I had worked in the ED, the ICU, had done staff education, and was an adjunct faculty member. I was persistent and kept moving on, trying to be positive. And then, finally, it happened; I got a callback and was offered a job with higher pay to head my own department at the Veterans Hospital in Arkansas.

My advice to anyone looking for a job is to be persistent and believe in yourself. I would say 60 percent of people in the world are in jobs they don't like. You have to look at what you enjoy doing and go after it. It's not always the job that pays the most money or the job your family wants you to have. It has to be the job you want, and you have to be persistent and go for it. Step out of your comfort zone.

໒໐

CHAPTER 19

It's Not You: It's the Job

BeBe's Story
Client Account Manager

I didn't expect to be laid off. I knew that things weren't good in my department, but you never expect it until it happens. Then you're depressed. You just don't feel good and you wonder why. But you can't stop though, you have to keep going and try not to take it personally.

When I did start looking for jobs after being laid off, I had some self-doubt. I was confident in my interviews, but didn't get hired. You start wondering. It gets frustrating. I would do a self-assessment. I knew I was knowledgeable and marketable. I have a master's degree. Then I started thinking, maybe I didn't have the corporate image, but I had worked in corporate America before I was laid off. I think a lot of women think that about themselves—they're not sure if they have the right image, are afraid they're over-weight, or that they don't have the look. After going on a few interviews, I would think maybe I had said something wrong, talked too much, or that my résumé didn't look right.

What really gets me are the happy headhunters. They call you up and invite you in and tell you about all these jobs they have available. You go on the interviews, and nothing happens. It's really disappointing. I ask myself, why are they calling and talking about all these jobs if nothing is going to happen? Still, you don't give up. Eventually something will happen and that's what happened to me. I started asking around and talking to people I had worked with previously, and they asked around and put me in contact with other people. After a while, things started to look better, and I found my current job. Talking to people and getting their feel on the market is always helpful and encouraging. Sometimes your contacts can suggest things you might want to change on your résumé or do in an interview.

My advice to anyone looking for a job is to follow your passion. My passion is helping others. I would like to teach life skills to the disadvantaged. I would also like to help juveniles plan for the future, focusing on their goals. Many of them don't have the foundation and knowledge to be successful in life. They don't have it because their parents didn't have it. Hopefully, in another few years, I will be able to follow my passion and dream, using my current job as a springboard.

☙

CHAPTER 20

It Can Get Tough Before It Gets Easy

Dylan's Story
Entrepreneur/Independent Contractor/Investment Banker

Some time ago, I met this very talented mutual fund manager, though at the time I neither appreciated nor valued him as much I should have. Turns out, he was a legendary player in his industry and he had shared an old African saying that I still live by:

> "Every morning in Africa, the lion and the antelope
> rise and seek their breakfast.
> The lion knows it must outrun the slowest
> of antelopes, or surely it will starve.
> The antelope knows it must outrun the slowest
> of lions, or surely it will be eaten.
> It doesn't matter if you are a lion or an antelope,
> when the sun comes up, you better be running."

Over the last nine years, I have been laid off once, fired twice, lost one business (meaning I fired myself), and came to the end of a contract job. From those experiences I have grown to understand that sometimes it's the economy, sometimes it's the place, sometimes it's the job that's not your strong suit, and sometimes it's just bad luck.

I was an investment banker. I sold mortgages to Wall Street. I worked with mergers and acquisitions and underwrote credits for major companies (TJX, GE, Ryder Logistics, KLM Airlines, Apple & Eve Juices).

When I was laid off from my investment job, I started looking for work in areas I could apply my credit analysis and capital markets skills. I then studied the path of success needed for those roles. I quickly learned that I needed certain certifications: Chartered Financial Analyst (CFA—the local chapter is the Boston Security Analyst Society), Chartered Alternative Investment Analyst (CAIA), and the Financial Risk Management (FRM) exam (GARP—Global Association of Risk Managers, Northeast chapter). I joined these groups and started studying for the certifications. However, not having a job definitely took a toll on my family.

I am married and we have school-age children. My wife, a schoolteacher, had the only permanent job in our home. After nine months of floundering, post-business failure in 2008, I landed a temporary job assignment at a bank. Debts were high, unemployment was becoming a problem, family gatherings and holidays were becoming harder because people were too embarrassed to ask about my job prospects. My wife and I were at odds—to the point where it felt like we might get a divorce. It was ugly. Even when you get out of bed and the fight is over, I was still left every day (even now) with an enormous debt that would have driven most people to claim bankruptcy. My pride would never let me do that. I needed to pay back everyone in full. I am still working it off. I had borrowed from friends and family, so they were getting heat for my business failure. It was brutal. I'd get the evil eye at home and then get calls from family and friends far and wide who felt serious bitterness toward me. I felt like I had nowhere to go.

Over time, that changed.

I became very focused in my job search and created a schedule for myself.

I joined a gym for health benefits—both mental and physical. I knew that the health benefits would help me feel better about myself and help me lead a healthy lifestyle. I changed my diet, and began to eat fish and vegetables more frequently, while staying away from fried foods. As a result, I lost weight and improved my health dramatically—lower cholesterol, better LDLs, less impact from allergies, all translated to reduced stress and a stronger focus. The only time to exercise for me was very early in the morning before going to work on my temporary job assignment. So four, sometimes five times a week, I would get up at 4:30 a.m., get dressed, and go work out from 5 a.m. to 6 a.m. in order to be home in time for my wife to leave for her job. It was a tough sacrifice going to bed at 9 p.m. and being asleep by 9:30 p.m., so I could wake up in time for the gym. I spent an intense hour at the gym. After that, I would go right into getting ready, cleaning up the kitchen, getting the kids to the bus stop, making a low calorie lunch, and driving into work. I would sometimes stay after work and study or take practice exams or do them at home. By the time I got home, all I had time to do was eat, tuck the kids into bed, review my notes for an hour, and go to sleep. That was my routine. The weekends were packed at the library with small breaks of games and events that the kids were participating in—I spent the majority of my time studying.

Weekends also gave me some TV time, enough to catch a baseball or football game. Sometimes during the week, I might wind down the day with a little TV. However, I always made time for my family.

One major necessity in my job search was a support system. I found other unemployed people, mostly through networking support groups on LinkedIn, some professional groups at my local employment office, and the local CFA chapter I had joined. I learned quickly that despite my situation, we are all people and we all need the same thing. I bonded with many of the people in these groups while job searching. We called each other almost daily and shared job leads that we ourselves didn't want, and some that we did. We figured, better one of us score the job to help the rest of us than some stranger. Frankly, I felt comfortable competing against the individuals that I had bonded with and often shared insights from my interviews with them. By giving out more information, I got more information back and felt great trust.

I attended every meeting sponsored by the Boston Security Analyst Society during the first few months of my membership. Sometimes I was the first person at the meeting, which made it very easy to meet people because I was the only one in the room. These venues provided me with a very targeted audience to sell myself and build my network. I quickly made cards with my name, e-mail, skill set, and positions desired. I also included my picture on the cards. This made me instantly recognizable.

Every meeting for me had a goal or purpose. I usually went to these meetings with twenty or so target companies that fit my criteria. I knew what I wanted and where I wanted to be long-term, so I stuck to the plan. I also determined my value with all three certifications, and the value continued to climb with this par-ticular trifecta of certifications. My goal was to find the person two levels above the hiring manager that I wanted to work for. I was scouting out potential employment. Usually I would find a person that worked for the company; I would take their card, and later, via e-mail, thank them and offer to meet with them for a cup of coffee in exchange for helping them with something they needed. Almost every time when they agreed to meet, they offered to take my résumé and run it up to their manager. In my case, I knew that was suicide. To me, a résumé is an excuse to dismiss someone, especially in human resources. When a résumé is passed up from someone below, it usually results in circling back to the impersonal desk of HR.

When those contacts offered to take my résumé to their managers, I always said, "You know, I'd really appreciate more understanding of the structure. I am still exploring the roles at the company and how they fit with my skill set." After that, I would take the phone number, e-mail, or even just the name and call or write a letter to the senior person I was hoping to work for. In the letter I would explain my background and experience. This process would help identify my skills as they related to the company's problems. That helped to have the employer design a position for me.

Also during my job search, I did charitable work, which helped my ability to expand my network and feel human at the same time. I was always involved with organized charities, and through charitable work I have always experienced the gift that givers gain. It's the concept that by giving back you actually gain more. By being nice and helping someone else get on their feet, you empower yourself to soldier on instead of hiding under the sheets watching movies all day. I had always remembered the stories of the Holocaust and how the Jewish prisoners that actually survived the longest were the ones that gave up their daily bread rations to other inmates and went hungry. It was a truism that demonstrated how extending humanity at a time of high stress and feelings of hopelessness gave them the strength to carry on.

I expanded my definition of charity to include directly helping the people right next to me. I even found someone who was going through a divorce and unemployed. He too was going through a job transition. He was in a tough place. He lost his wife, kids, house, and two jobs, all in less than a year after hiding a three-year affair (with his true love). Although I couldn't identify with the affair, I knew exactly what it felt like to be a pariah. Regardless, I felt every kid needs a good father, and I had known him to be a good father. I knew I could help build him up, so I did. Since he did the primary work as the parent, I frequently saw him with his kids at sporting events for his children. Without him, I could tell the kids would be lost, as his ex-wife was not as interested in making sure they were active and involved. In the end, he took the high road in the divorce after realizing that he screwed up. He made it right. He changed his life and left his true love in New York and moved closer to his wife to be near his kids. In his case, without me, I knew he would be alone and maybe he would have made different choices. I stood by him and built him up for the things he did right and reassured his value to his kids and his ability to do a good job. Sometimes I bought him lunch or paid for a beer, because I knew he needed to blow off steam, and I could still afford to pay for it. He is now building his own business in structured settlements while working from home. As for his true love, he is back in contact with her. For me, this small contribution made me feel human. I gave my bread, so to speak, to someone less fortunate. As a result, I learned that helping others also helps minimize the hurt factor of job rejection.

In the end, I manage to pull myself up. Now, I am about to join a Spanish bank, so I bought a program to teach me how to speak Spanish. The overall lesson from my first experience of unemployment to my most recent is that I now know what is required to move up in my industry. You just can't go at it the old way, which was to write a letter, write a résumé, and submit them through the company website and wait for an answer. For me, that was never going to work. I also needed to demonstrate continued learning and improvement. I am convinced that my changed perspective is what got me hired.

∽

CHAPTER 21

From Stay-At-Home Dad to Working Dad

Chris's Story
Chemical Packing Plant From the Midwest

When I think I have it bad, I always ask myself what would Jesus do? What would Jesus say? Then I tell God that I am thankful for what I have and what I have not. I also remember there are those who have less and are suffering more than I. I then ask to be forgiven for my selfish ways and ask for his guidance.

I was unemployed from September 2008 until June 14, 2010. The company I worked for called it a permanent layoff. At first it sucked. I thought the end of the world was coming. I had to keep busy doing things around the house (special projects, building things, gardening) because there were no jobs, not even at fast food places, nearby. There were mostly factories, as we are in a beltway community. I think the most important thing you need to get by in a situation like this economy is God first, family second, and a lot of friends third.

It really helps to have a spouse who is supportive and understanding. My wife and I have been married fifteen years now and I will have to say she is my best friend, and the best wife a man could ask for.

When I lost my job, we had to give up our vacation plans to go to Disney World that year, which was sad. I had been before with my parents when I was young, and I really wanted to take my children, but we just didn't have the money. That Christmas everyone got one gift. We were unable to exchange gifts with other family members, for many of them had also lost their jobs. Our kids were great. They understood, thankfully, that we wouldn't be able to exchange gifts. Normally we would spend one to two thousand dollars on gifts. With the new job, we only spend two hundred fifty dollars on gifts.

One of my projects when I wasn't working was writing for CNN's iReport. I stumbled on iReport about six or eight months before I lost my job and didn't really know what to do or say on iReport at the time. It was months later, when I lost my job, that I started posting because I was on the Internet searching for jobs. The stories that I posted were about the bad economy in the Midwest and the lack of jobs. Posting stories on iReport allowed me to hear the stories of other people who were looking for jobs. Reading the stories of people who were in the same boat made me feel better. It was a feeling I had never felt before. It was kinda crazy…and twisted that you could feel better knowing others were hurting like you.

Eventually, I landed a job at a chemical repack plant that is about fifteen minutes away, on the outskirts of the town where I live. I didn't even know it existed. I have been there since June 14, 2010. Believe it or not, now I have a prospect for a job at a paper mill about ten minutes away from where I live. The pay is twice the amount I am making now, so I am pretty excited.

Looking back on everything, I think the hardest thing about going back into the workforce is the kids (ten and thirteen). They didn't want me to go. They liked having a stay-at-home dad, but they understood that if they wanted to go to college, I needed to work.

෬

CHAPTER 22

Prepare Yourself by Downsizing

Elizabeth's Story
Elementary Teacher/Medical Student/Healthcare Administrator

I would advise anyone who is dissatisfied with his/her current employment and not independently wealthy to start preparing to downsize your life. This will be most beneficial in the transition to the desired state of employment, such as your dream job. Start by paying off all or most of your debt, and do not make any new purchases. Do whatever it takes or make whatever sacrifices you need to make to get yourself in a position where you can leave your current job and not end up starving and/or homeless. This will allow you the leeway to move forward with your plans with the least amount of stress because, as we all know, uncertain finances can cause mega stress.

I did just that. I was a classroom teacher for many years in the South. I enjoyed teaching, but was not a fan of the politics involved. While teaching, I went back to school and got a graduate degree in counseling psychology. Then my husband got a job in the Midwest and moved our family there, where I returned to school to study medicine. I had always wanted to be a doctor and thought, why not now? I completed a post baccalaureate and was accepted into medical school. However, juggling family life and medical school with no support proved to be too much. My children and husband wanted me home. So I took a break from school, but the desire was still there.

The funny thing is that once my children were grown up and I was in a position to return to medical school, I realized that I really didn't want to invest the time and money anymore. However, I wanted to stay in medicine, and that is how I ended up in cancer research, which fulfills my need to work in medicine and help others.

I have always enjoyed writing fiction and as an added bonus, my job allows me to time to write and be creative as well. The ability to take a blank page and fill it with thought-provoking, meaningful words is amazing to me. Now I get to live my dream life. The only thing missing is to be published, which will come soon. Yes, you must always think positive.

၈၁၀

CHAPTER 23

Reinvent Yourself for the Job

Todd's Story
Broker/Computer Software Tech/Compliance Officer

I've been working since I was fourteen and have been laid off and fired. Each time I was laid off or fired, it hurt. You're never prepared for it. Sometimes you see it coming and others times you don't. You take it personally because you're human, but you have to put it into perspective.

As a teenager I worked in a mall for a tobacco store. One day, one of the store's regular customers came in and wanted a cigar, but he didn't have money. Because he was a regular customer and good guy, I gave him the cigar and told him he could bring the money in when he got it. When my boss found out what I had done, he didn't like it. In fact, he fired me. I was pissed because I felt slighted. I thought what I had done was good customer service. He said I was naïve. On another occasion, I was working at a gadget store and wanted to go hang out with friends. I told my manager I needed to leave early. He said no. I lied and said I had a stomachache and left. My manager found out and fired me. I even got fired from Kinney

Shoes when I was a teenager. Each time I was fired, I felt like a complete failure and took it personally. As an adult I've been fired, laid off, and asked to resign. And even as an adult, the sting is still there and it hurts. Though I've learned not to take it so personally, it's hard not to. Something else—each time I lost a job, I now realized the job or jobs weren't for me. Either I wasn't growing in the position, the salary was low, the working conditions were horrible, or my boss had it in for me. Once I accepted the firing or layoff, I became empowered, reinvented myself, and got a better job.

I personally think too many people stay in jobs they don't like because they're afraid to leave. They have tunnel vision and get caught up in the company culture. They think the job is their life and all they have, but there is more out there. You have to take a risk. If your job isn't working out, don't be afraid to look for something else. It's not like the old days where you work for a company that you don't like until you retire. Look at yourself as a free agent. If things aren't working out, it's time to take control of your career and go somewhere else. Staying at a job you don't like will only make you miserable. Another thing to think about is that the job you are trying to hold onto could be trying to get rid of you. I had two jobs like this. DH Blair, a broker firm, where I was a cold caller and at *The PennySaver* newspaper, where I sold ads. Both jobs were awful, but they paid the bills. In the case of DH Blair, they wouldn't fire you. The company just made your life so miserable that you would quit, and quit I did. Then there was *The PennySaver*. I would get sick in my stomach the day before going to work. I wasn't any good at selling ads and never met my numbers. I lasted for nine months and was relieved when it was over.

My first serious job after college was as a licensed broker for Charles Schwab. I was really excited about the job when I started in New York, but after several months, my boss decided she didn't like me for whatever the reason. I did everything I could to make her like me, but it just wasn't happening. This made my first three years on the job awful. This woman did everything she could to get me fired. I guess she didn't like that I was doing a good job and popular with the clients and senior management. I started hating coming into work. She would do little things to get at me. Some bosses are like that—they'll target you and try to make your life miserable, either because they are threatened or they get a feeling of power out of inflicting misery on another person. Lucky for me, she ended up being fired and I stayed on and things got better. After several years in one position, I transferred to the Denver, Colorado office. I really liked the job in Denver. I was good at it, but after several years, it wasn't exactly fulfilling. Because the atmosphere had gotten better for me, I got caught up in the company culture. I had made friends. The salary was good and I felt comfortable. After a while, I got bored and decided to resign and move back home to New York to be closer to my family.

Once I returned to New York, I started working for a buddy of mine. He owned a car repair shop. I worked as a gopher doing a little of everything. I got coffee for the mechanics, answered the phone, moved cars. A regular blue-collar job. While this guy was my friend, the job didn't work out because the black and white terms of my employment weren't honored. There were gray areas. Sometimes he would pay me, and other times he wouldn't. When I was paid, it was partial pay. He felt that because we were friends I would be okay with partial or late pay. It's really hard working for a friend, and our friendship grew strained. So I decided to quit to keep the friendship from going completely south. Now things are okay between us again.

After working for my buddy, I decided to reenter corporate America. I went to work for TD Waterhouse, as a cold caller. I didn't like this job at all. Both the salary and potential bonus pools were horrible. In addition to bringing in investments, one of the conditions of employment was to pass an exam. I lasted all of six months before they let me go. The company gave me the option of resigning or being fired. I knew that if I resigned, I wouldn't qualify for unemployment, but if they fired me it would have gone on my broker U four form. I made the decision to be fired and was relieved to put the job behind me. Some jobs just aren't meant to be—not that my next job at a software company was any better.

I don't know how I got the job and lasted as long as I did. I had no background in computer programming. I have a degree in economics and was completely unqualified for the job. Somehow I managed to talk my way through the interview and sounded as though I knew what I was talking about. When I was offered the job, I was shocked but accepted. I needed the money. The first day on the job, I was in over my head. I would be sitting in meetings, listening to all these technical terms and techno-jargon being thrown around. Whenever they asked my thoughts on something, I would repeat what was said, shake my head in agreement, and they bought it. Deep down inside me I knew it was a matter of time before it caught up with me, but I figured by then I would have another job. I lasted for six months before my boss, whose office was in San Diego, started to figure it out. I can't forget that day. I was on a conference call and started spacing out. Out of the blue I was asked a question and I didn't know how to answer—it caught me completely off guard. That was the decisive point for my boss. After the meeting, he came up to me and asked me to write a technical software manual for a client. I tried to get out of it by saying that I wasn't a technical writer and that I was hired as a go-between the program designers and clients. I knew this was a set-up; it was their way of managing me out of the company. He gave me a guide to use as a format and said I needed to have it done in thirty days. I knew then I had thirty days to get another job. So I spent half of each day at work writing the guide and the other half looking for a job. I also made use of the time to remove all my personal belongings from the office—not that I had much. I worked hard on the manual and my job search. A week shy of the thirty days, my boss's boss called me into his office. I thought to myself, *this is it*. I went to his office and he closed the door and sat at his desk with his back toward me. He had my boss on speakerphone, and they started drilling me about the manual. I had already sent my boss a copy of the manual for review. Those moments in the office were brutal. My boss started questioning me about things he didn't see in the manual. I responded by giving him specific page numbers to refer to. He then literally started to pick apart the manual. Throughout this time his boss, who had been at his desk, never turned around to look at me. He was busy on his computer. Finally, after the interrogation was over, my boss hung up the phone and his boss turned to me and said things weren't working out, and I wasn't the right fit. So I was asked to leave. I was so mad. When I left his office and returned to my desk, my laptop and client files had been removed. I found out later on that during my meeting, my boss's boss, who had spent the entire time on his computer, was busy communicating with office staff to remove my laptop and other office files. The only satisfaction I got from all this is that I threw my boss under the bus. I told his boss before leaving that the guy had poor management skills and wasn't focused. In hindsight, I probably should have just left without taking digs at my boss. After all, staying at a job I wasn't qualified to do for six months was a feat in itself.

After the software job, I reinvented myself and focused on my knowledge of risk and compliance that I had gained during my time with Schwab. I contacted a few headhunters and entered the world of consulting.

My first consulting job in compliance went well. The pay was great and the people were friendly, but like all consulting assignments, it had a beginning and end date. Shortly afterward, I landed the job of a lifetime with a major financial firm on Wall Street. This job was permanent. It was ideal salary-wise, with a great bonus structure, and I was managing a team of twenty people. We were working on a high-level anti-money-laundering project that had two deadlines. Finally, I thought, I had made it. I had the right group of people to help me complete the project, and I was confident it would get done. Again, it's always the first year that gets you sold on the job, and my first year was great. I was able to complete the first year of the project with two years left. But after the first year or so, things started to change. The guy who hired me left. I then found myself reporting to two project managers and another guy who thought he was my boss, but was actually a neurotic peer.

I don't care how much you like your boss, always remember that your boss could leave, and while you can't always follow your boss around or quit a job because your boss has left, if the environment at work changes, I say get out. That's what happened to me at my ideal job. I had the job for five years and I tried to stay longer, but for every good year there was a bad one after my first boss left. It seemed like every day there was a change in direction.

Every minute and hour I was given a directive to change processes in the way my team worked. It was crazy but manageable. Two managers giving me instructions with this third leg, who knew nothing, in the background trying to give me orders. I didn't have to worry about him for long because he was asked to leave the project. You would have thought things would have settled down after that, but they didn't. A few months after his departure, the company placed a senior manager over my two immediate managers. From that point, things really started going downhill. It was only a matter of time before my immediate managers, whom I had worked well with, resigned, one after the other. They said they had gotten better opportunities. I was left me behind with the new project manager who was a complete control freak and narcissist. He was all over the map with his instructions. My job became completely confusing and the stress level high. With all of that, I still managed to keep my team on target to complete the project. As we neared the end of the project, it became evident that my remaining days with the project weren't going to end well. And wouldn't you know it, another manager came in to supervise it and the narcissist was out. This guy seemed to know what he was doing. I breathed a sigh of relief, but before he could get his feet wet, he was moved to another division of the firm. And the narcissist was back in the picture. I began dreading coming into work. This guy was making things so unbearable. I often wondered if my first two managers left because this guy was such a control freak. He challenged me on everything. There was a lot of "guilty until proven innocent" with him. When things went well on the project, he took credit. When anything went wrong, he would look to blame me or my team. It was extremely frustrating. This guy was the manager you have nightmares about. There were meetings every day and every minute about the same thing we had met on previously. Believe it or not, we would have a meeting about the meeting and then another meeting. This was literally every day. I often wondered how he managed to make it so far in his career. This craziness went on right up to the month of the project's completion date, which was my final day of work. Yet another day I won't forget. The guy calls me into his office to discuss my staff, but when I got there, I saw that he had invited an HR rep. I knew then that something else was going to be discussed.

Once you realize you are going to be laid off or fired, you should start looking. That is exactly what I did. I knew it was only a matter of time before my narcissist manager would let me go. He couldn't afford to keep me around. That would have meant sharing in the project's completion. While I expected him to let me go, I was still pissed. All the work I put into the project—gone. I had assembled the right staff and we were near the finish line, and he pulled me out. Thankfully though, I was able to keep my bonus with a severance package.

If your boss doesn't like you, don't waste your time trying to change his or her mind. It won't happen. Don't waste your time trying to convince someone that you are a good guy and should be liked. Once your boss has made up his mind that he doesn't like you and feels threatened, the wheels are in motion to get you out. The best thing you can do for yourself is to plan an exit strategy and stay on long enough to get a severance package while looking for another job. Now, you can always stand up to your boss and take jabs, but is it worth it?

When I look back at my career, I have learned not to lose my identity in a job. I have always taken risks in my careers and will continue to do so. I strongly believe that if a job isn't working, leave. You have to view yourself as a free agent and not be afraid to reinvent yourself. There is always something better out there for you. You simply have to empower yourself to do better and get better. Believe in yourself. That's what I have always done.

つ

CHAPTER 24

The Formula for Success is Persistence

Raymond's Story
RL Hinton, P.C.Atlanta, Georgia

I read somewhere that the late Estelle Getty, who played Sophia in the Golden Girls, used to quit or refuse promotions when she worked as a secretary. This was before she started acting. She did this because she didn't want to lose sight of her dream of becoming an actress. She got her start late in life, but she knew what she wanted. She followed her passion. Some people would look at her decision to stay and say she was crazy. I see it as her not getting secure and comfortable.

It's a natural human instinct to want security. Many of us find security in a job. Most of the time it's a job we don't like, but it's security and gives us comfort. But what good is being comfortable if you're not happy with what you do? We spend the majority of our time at work. I want to be doing something I enjoy as opposed to just being comfortable with a job I don't like. Realizing this fact is easier said than done, but what's the alternative? Settling for a job you don't like, and then retiring with regrets? Retirement isn't promised. You could die before your retirement. Life is so fragile; there are no guarantees in life. Not only that, but today's job market is full of uncertainty. Companies are constantly laying people off. Very few people stay at one job and retire with the same company. Even if you want to retire with a company, it might not be possible. Companies nowadays don't even keep the same workforce for five or ten years. Individuals lucky enough to stay with a company until retirement are usually so miserable that when they retire they aren't happy. Ask yourself, *when I retire, will I have regrets with the choices and paths taken today?* Another way of looking at the same question is to fast-forward to your retirement. What would you like to be able to say for the years you worked for company X? Were you there because you liked it, or were you there just to pay the bills and float through life? If you can't answer those questions with certainty, then you should start looking at making changes in your life. Don't be afraid. Once you realize your passion, go for it. Be careful not to fall for the comfort jobs you take to get you to your passion. View these jobs as stepping-stones.

Pacific Bell was my secure, comfortable job. I was one of two CPAs working in internal audit. The company was generous with pay and was paying for my MBA at Pepperdine. I looked forward to going to work, and it was easy. Little did I know when I was hired that the department was in the middle of a reorganization. Internal audit was considered a graveyard at Pacific. They were trying to change that image. All the mess-ups in other parts of the company were sent there, including my boss. In the beginning, the job was great. I had thought it was too good to be true, and then the politics started. My salary was frozen and then I was demoted and had to report to auditors who were formerly my peers, which was humiliating. When talks of layoffs surfaced, my boss told me he would lay me and the other CPA off before laying anyone else off. He figured it would easier for us to find jobs than the others on the team. So, there I was, at a job that I really liked, but one that didn't care for me. Soon I grew to dislike the job. I voiced my dissatisfaction with how things were going many times, but nothing was done. I told myself I would try and stick it out until I got my MBA, but that proved to be a challenge because my boss wanted me to move to our office in Northern California. My boss indicated that for me to have a future with the company, I would need to move. It was understood that I would transfer after completing my MBA. But I had no intention of moving. After getting my degree and being given the ultimatum to transfer to Northern California or be demoted again, I tendered my resignation. Shortly after I left, the Pacific was bought by SBC Communications, headquartered in Austin, and then AT&T, which is headquartered in Dallas.

The Pacific Bell experience made me realize that just like life, tomorrow is not promised. I couldn't depend on a job where I couldn't control my fate. This fact made me passionate about working for myself and controlling my fate. This led me to incorporate myself and create my own CPA firm.

Starting out was slow but gradually I started to build my client base. However, in the process of growing my business, I got a divorce, and my ex-wife and daughter moved to Atlanta. To be near my daughter, I moved to Atlanta. Needless to say, my business took a hit once clients realized I wasn't in Los Angeles. Until I grew the business in Atlanta, I took a job as tax manager with a private company. My salary from this job was going to be used to build capital to put into my business. Again, another job that was ideal and sweet. I saw myself staying there for three or four years. There was so much for me to learn. The company was small and everyone seemed friendly. Right after I came on board, my supervisor went on a personal leave. While she was gone I was tasked with auditing all the books and making their systems automated—an easy task. Things started going south when my supervisor returned. I was over-qualified for the job. I had an MBA, was a CPA, and had a plethora of experience at some of the largest accounting firms. After eighteen months of being on the job, I was let go along with several other employees, including executives.

In hindsight, I believe I was hired solely to maintain the company while my supervisor took a personal leave.

Thankfully the firing didn't stop me. It made me more determined to grow my business and work for myself. This all happened around the time the economy was taking a downturn in 2008. Since then, I have managed to replenish my business with clients and continue to grow. I didn't give up. I was persistent.

Pacific Bell and this private company both taught me valuable lessons. Always try to learn something new from the job. Depending on the time you are with the company, go back to school to further your education (as long as they pay). This will make you more marketable to future employers. Lastly, never let a job get in the way of your passion.

There's always the temptation to stay on a job that isn't into you because of security. Often times what you are getting from the job salary, retirement benefits, and money in the bank will cause you to ignore the job not being into you. Had things not gone the way they had at Pacific Bell, I probably wouldn't have left.

Looking back, I'm glad I took the chances I have taken to get to where I am. I say to all entrepreneurs and college students leaving school now who can't find a job: now is the time to do whatever it is you are passionate about. You may not have this chance again. How much can you lose chasing a dream with a company and not knowing your fate or following your own passion and controlling your outcome?

Before my father died, he was a successful engineer and the first black to graduate from Oklahoma University. He always told me that he wished he had dreamed bigger in life, aimed higher. I guess he thought there was a ceiling on how far he could go and there really wasn't, but he only realized it after he retired.

∽

CHAPTER 25

An Unlikely Career

Tatyana's Story
Mechanical Engineer/Consultant

I wanted to be a ballerina.

I loved the arts, singing, music, and dancing. I especially loved to dance, and studied dance as a child growing up in Russia. I was accepted to a musical school for talented children in St. Petersburg. When I completed my intermediate studies, my plan was to enter school and study the humanities—languages, art, history, or music. My parents, who were both doctors, thought otherwise. They didn't see a future for me in those areas. How could I make money studying language or art? They saw me studying science and becoming a doctor instead. I didn't want to be a doctor, for I was squeamish about human anatomy, especially human dissection.

I had always been good at numbers. My grandmother was a schoolteacher and lived with my parents and me. She taught me my numbers and to read at an early age. By the time I was three I was doing arithmetic and made good grades throughout school. Engineering was a logical choice. I gave in to my parents and studied engineering at Polytechnical Institute in Latvia. After completing my degree, I became an engineer. I worked as an engineer until my husband moved our family to the United States in 1990. In the United States, my degree didn't carry much weight, so I had to reinvent myself. Knowing very little English and having no marketable skills, I had to start from scratch. It wasn't easy. My husband and I had very little money and two small children. Not wanting to leave my children (ages eight and three) with babysitters, I stayed at home with them. To learn the language and keep busy, I would help elderly residents in the building where we lived. These little old ladies would engage me in conversations and I would listen, trying to get the courage to speak. There was one nice lady I remember in particular. She was ninety-four years old and though her body was weak, she had a sharp mind. She had come to the states from Germany at the age of forty. She helped me learn the language. She would have long conversations with me and encourage me to talk. Eventually, I found my voice.

It took me two and a half years to prepare myself for reentry to the workforce. By then I was comfortable with the language and had taught myself word processing: Microsoft Office and Lotus Notes. I sent my résumé to a temporary agency on John Street in lower Manhattan. They called me in had me take several tests and sent me out on a temporary job assignment the following week. My first job was a clerical position with the American Stock Exchange. Once the job was over, I received a call from the same agency about my availability for another assignment. I said I was available. Then I was asked if I knew the alphabet. I was shocked when asked because this same agency had sent me out on my initial assignment. I answered yes to the question but was then asked to recite the alphabet. I did. When I was done speaking with the agency, I hung up the phone. I started crying and told my husband what happened. Being an educated woman, I was so hurt. This agency knew nothing about me and I was being treated as though I was nobody—all for a job as a filing clerk. But I knew why the agency wanted to know if I knew the alphabet. It's because some internationals come to the U.S. and say they understand the language but don't. I said to my husband that I wasn't going to accept the job. He then reminded me that I had said I would do any job to give my children a better future and a chance to leave Russia. I accepted the position. I did a great job and got to know many of the hiring managers there. Right before the assignment was up, the general counsel asked my agency to extend my contract.

After contracting for a while, I landed a full-time position with an investment firm on Wall Street.

Were any of these my dream jobs or jobs that allowed me to follow my passion? They were jobs that I needed and got. I am enjoying my life in corporate America considering what it took me to get there. By no means had I planned a life in corporate America, but I am grateful for it.

Even now I think about my dream of being a ballerina. In the past I have gone to see Ulyana Lopatkina perform at the Met. Ulyana is a principal dancer at the Kirov Ballet Mariinsky Theatre in St. Petersburg, Russia. She is so beautiful—long and elegant. Whenever she comes to the States, I go see her perform. She is beautiful.

I feel as though I could have been a famous ballerina.

༄

CHAPTER 26

Leave Your Job With Grace

Barbara's Story
Advertising/Mortgages/Hiring Manager

If you are independently wealthy, you can leave a job and go after your passion.

It's easy to tell someone to get out of a job that isn't into them. The person doing the telling has nothing to lose. The reality is nine out of ten people who should and probably want to leave their job because they hate it, can't do it. You get sucked into the job. You are receiving a steady pay (it may not be the best), you have vacation time, and you're comfortable. At one point, I had wanted to be in advertising. I was told by a college professor that I had a knack for it, but years of being in finance caused me to move in a different direction. I stayed in finance. Most people get jobs they really don't like but that are convenient. You don't plan to stay, but you do—until something better comes along or the company lets you go. The latter option isn't so great.

If you are let go, as hard as it is not to, don't take it personally. Leave with your dignity intact. Say *thank you for the opportunity* and leave. You never want to make a scene or burn bridges that you may have to cross later. Keep your head held high and walk out without crying. Besides, if you are working for a good company, I'm sure it wasn't easy for them to make the decision to lay you off, and they probably thought of other jobs that might suit you. I know this firsthand

When I was a hiring manager at Paine Webber in New Jersey, I had to fire one of my employees. I hated it. I did everything possible to keep from firing her. She was young, bright, and knew her stuff. Unfortunately, she had a few personality issues with other workers, and the job really wasn't for her. One day there was a major blow-up in the office in front of clients, and my manger told me to let her go. I danced around my orders and tried to avoid it. I had a soft spot for her and felt awful thinking I would be the person delivering the news. Because our office was a satellite, there wasn't an HR person available to come in and deliver the news. The day I let her go was not good. It got ugly and I got sick. From that day on, I told myself I never wanted to manage people.

If you happen to get laid off or fired, rely on your contacts from previous jobs to help you look for a new job. They are always good sources. At the same time, you should explore other avenues, especially if you want to go after your passion. Reinventing yourself isn't always easy, but don't give up. You have to be determined. Your ideal job may not come immediately. I used to encourage colleagues who were in dead-end jobs to move on. I remember telling one guy I worked with everyday that he was in the wrong job and he should pursue his dreams. I'm sure he thought I was crazy, but he eventually took my advice and now he couldn't be any happier. As for me, I am still looking for my ideal job, and I won't stop until I find it. It's never too late.

∾

CHAPTER 27

You Never Know When the Music Will Stop

Linda Marie's Story
Banker/Entrepreneur/Credit Officer

Employment is like musical chairs. You never know when the music stops and you're the one left without a chair.

You can be set up to succeed or set up to fail. I didn't recognize until too late that I had been set up to fail at my job. I had been a highly successful banker. I was well known throughout the organization. My boss was great and he valued my opinions. Although we were in two different offices, we were always in contact during the workweek, bouncing ideas off one another. I had two great years with him before things started to change. This seems to be the norm in corporate America. You have a few good years, and then things change. With me it was the merger of our bank with another. For me this meant more work and minimal support staff, but I managed. Soon I was offered a different position at a higher level, using my expertise in credit and lending. I was also told that I would have appropriate support to do the job. I saw this as a great opportunity and accepted the position. Little did I know that I wouldn't be getting the support they promised.

First, the support staff I was promised was scratched, including my personal assistant. I would have to do everything on my own. While I wasn't too happy about that, I was willing to adapt. But then, by some strange twist of fate, my reporting line changed. I would now be reporting to an individual in another office and state and at my level. The person was my equal but minus my expertise and knowledge. I didn't like this—it felt awkward. Here I was, reporting to some guy who didn't have my skills or accomplishments under his belt and had no vested interest in my success. I had nothing against the guy. He was bright, but weak in what he was doing. Not confident in himself. I was now reporting to someone who I might one day have to compete with. Initially I had thought to say something, but with the merger, there really wasn't anyone in the new work structure for me to express my concerns. Had I gone up a few levels and said something, I imagined the tsunami that followed would have been unbearable career-wise. My only option was to adapt. Accept what seemed like an unfair break, but try to work within the job's structure. The first few months I tried to adapt, but it was nearly impossible. I was in the New York office and my team was in North Carolina. I didn't have some of the most basic things I needed, like computer access and passwords, policy and process flow. I didn't have regular contact with my team or my boss. I would reach out to my boss by phone, by e-mail, and receive nothing back. No one would return my calls. They were like a goon squad. I needed to be kept in the loop, but I wasn't.

I was furious, and I knew what was happening. I was being isolated and made to look incompetent. I tried in the beginning to be super patient, not to lose my cool. I kept sending e-mails and making phone calls to figure out the system to do my job.

Soon I realized I had accepted a job that had morphed into something completely different from what I had signed on to do.

The company directors in New York were new and unknown to me. They were, however, known to the management team that put me in this situation. It became obvious to me I was being set up to fail. All at once I felt alone. There was never was a real chance for me in the new position. Still, I kept telling myself to do my best, keep working, and be professional. Months later, after being on the team of "no contact," I was given a project that I call "sudden death." It had to be done quickly. Even with the obstacles I was facing, I quickly completed the project of writing a credit proposal for a client. My boss, on the other hand, took two, maybe three weeks to get back to me. He knew people were waiting for the project to be completed, but this was a way of saying I held it up, even though he was the one sitting on it. I was proactive and called and e-mailed him to see where he was in the process of reviewing it. He didn't respond. I knew then this would be indicative of his behavior for the rest of my time on the team. Once he finally read the proposal, he contacted me and said it was okay, but he needed to make some changes. At first, I didn't think much of him making changes. While we were both on the phone, he started going through it line by line—it was wordsmithery of the worst kind. It was obvious he was only rearranging my words. My sentence read ABC, and he would redo it to read CBA. I called this to his attention. He got all choked up and said that I had used incorrect grammar, and that it was his responsibility to correct it. I knew he didn't have an idea what he was doing. On another occasion, while reviewing a different proposal I asked if he was going to "correct my grammar"—if so, I didn't want to be on the phone while he did it. I suggested he make the changes and send them to me via e-mail. We then went back and forth a few times about why he wouldn't agree to making the changes off the phone. I was so exasperated by then that I said, "I get it. You just want me to shut up so you can abuse this situation."

He sighed and said, "I would like to finish the memo please."

I said "Fine. Finish and send it to me." To spend time reordering my sentences for a proposal was just ball-busting. I thought to myself the last time someone edited my grammar was in high school. My professional career was about concept issues and numbers, not sentence structure. After that, my boss and I didn't speak for a while, not that we had been speaking on a regular basis before.

Finally when the silence was broken, I was labeled a difficult employee. My boss claimed to have interviewed my team members and other colleagues and there were complaints that I was difficult to work with and rude. These charges and other infractions were all spelled out in a meeting with my boss and his boss. I was considered someone who had issues working with colleagues, as well as performance issues. I listened to him as he read the charges. Now, this was coming from a guy who hardly spoke to me and who had little to no contact with me or my team, as we worked in different offices and in different states. My only contact with my boss was by phone which was pretty much nonexistent. After the charges were read, I asked if I could say something in my defense. I made a few comments about being surprised to hear such accusations. I then asked if I could think about what had been said and get back to them to discuss it further. At the time, I just wanted the meeting to be over; I was so disgusted. They then asked if I was willing to work with my peers. I knew then no matter what I said, they were telling me I had done something wrong. Though I had done nothing wrong, I was guilty in their eyes.

To resolve what was perceived as a problem, my workload was restructured and reporting lines changed. I was told I would be reporting to yet another peer but in the same office as me. Once this decision was made, my boss wanted my assurance that I would accept the change and work with my colleagues. I was speechless; I knew that I had done nothing wrong. I was the person constantly trying to adapt to the entire work environment independently. My phone calls went unreturned and my e-mails unanswered. The

responses that I did get from my team were always nasty, but I
tried to keep my cool. From the very beginning, if I said it was
black, they said white. This seems to be the pattern when someone
is being managed to fail. Everything you say is challenged. In the
end, because my boss felt threatened by my earlier successes, I knew
there was nothing more I could do. I said to myself, *I can resign now
or end the conversation and think about my next steps.* To their question
of working with my colleagues, I answered yes. What more could
I have said?

A month later, I requested a leave of absence. Later I relin-
quished my position but stayed with the company.

In hindsight, I realize adapting in my situation was not going
to work. I didn't know it at the time. The entire matter was demor-
alizing to say the least, but that happens in corporate America. One
day you are managing and the next day the person you were reviewing is now your manager. It's like a revolving door.

In a good working situation, you have a respectful boss and you
are encouraged and given opportunities to grow. Your talents are
recognized and appreciated. These are all traits of a good boss and
work environment. Without either, you can't grow. You are miserable and you have to leave for brighter and better things or all the
good things in you will dry up. You have to decide, before the job
does, that you're just not into it.

In retrospect, when I look at all that I have done in my life,
had I to do it all over, I would have majored in creative writing or
literature—anything but business. Growing up, my dream was to
be a journalist or research psychologist. I enjoy writing and being
creative. I can read books on psychology all night long, though I
would probably vomit if I had to read a business book all night. I
guess I didn't pursue my dream jobs because my family was nervous about careers ending with "ist." My dad, an assistant principal,
and mother, a teacher, favored solid careers in fields like nursing,
teaching, and accounting. These were jobs they felt were grounded.

This is typical of my parents' generation. Their upbringing stressed the importance of education as preparation for a professional career. I sucked it up and went into finance. In college, professors were advising students to go into business and get a degree, which then seemed to be the thing for women who weren't represented in corporate America. I completed my bachelor's degree and went on to pursue an MBA. It was the smart thing to do for women. You were making an excellent career choice that put you in a position to break the glass ceiling. Only smart women were doing it. However, had I done a little more introspection I probably would have asked instead, *What does Linda really love to do?* So I got the MBA, was considered smart, and entered the world of banking. I was recruited to work for a major Wall Street bank. I was on the fast track to being a successful independent woman in the world of finance and I was having a good time. Still, the creative side of me was longing to make its presence known, but I didn't know how to let it flourish. It then dawned on me to open a clothing store. On the side, I had been working with friends who owned a fashion boutique. With their help and encouragement, I opened my own. The boutique allowed the creative side of me to come out. It was a business venture that allowed me to be creative while using my financial acumen. It was fun traveling to the Paris fashion shows as a buyer and knowing about all the latest trends. I had the store for eighteen months before closing it. There wasn't enough profit. Some months were strong, some dead. I felt it would be too long before I could fully devote myself to the business. Shortly after the closing, I took two years off to get my master's and work on my PhD before I burned out. I then came back to finance.

Even after coming back to finance, at various times I thought it would be nice to do something else. But where can I make this kind of money, mainly in bonuses? In the finance world, you are working for the bonus and not the salary. That's how they get you. You're paid well. You enjoy it and your spending power increases. If I had left to go work for a newspaper, I estimated my salary would have dropped considerably from the six figures I was making and I doubt there would have been a bonus. I couldn't see myself working for such little money.

Now I am at a place in my life where I am happy. I am attempting to revisit my creative side. I know now when something is to be and when it isn't.

๏~๏

CHAPTER 28

Flying With My Dream

Kenny G's Story
Insurance Claims Adjuster/Personal Trainer/Model/
Business Owner/ Airline Pilot

Most people have three walls, a door, and a window for an office. I have the entire sky as my office. Looking out my window brings me a different view every day.

Growing up on a military base in Texas, I was surrounded by airplanes and pilots. During the summer, I would sit outside all day and watch the planes take off. It was the coolest thing to me. I imagined being in the big blue sky among the clouds and watching the world. I knew then that's what I wanted to be—a pilot. My dream, however, was crushed when my dad told me that I needed 20/20 vision (which was the military standard) to fly a plane, and I wore glasses. Back then, Google wasn't around, so I had no way of searching the Internet to determine if what my dad was saying was true, not that I didn't believe him. I mean, he was my dad and a military guy. I believed him, and he was right. The qualification for military pilots was 20/20 vision, but not for commercial pilots. Anyway, I put my dream aside, went to college, got a degree in business management, graduated, and became an insurance adjuster for State Farm in Colorado.

I can't say that I loved the job, but I did like the benefits it gave me. I bought my first house and a second home before I was thirty. I always loved dogs, so I bought the pet of my dreams— a Doberman pinscher. I named her Nayla. I went on vacations, bought a sports car, and was living the life of a bachelor. That grew old after nine years. Something was missing. I didn't feel complete. Ha! My dream of wanting to fly planes was still in the pit of my stomach. But it was out of my reach because I didn't have 20/20 vision (or so I had thought). What came next? Well, of all things, I decided to try my luck at being a male model. I know it sounds strange, but many of my girlfriends told me I had the looks. Even some of my clients joked around with me and said I should be a model. So I thought, what the heck? You only live once. Why not? I resigned from my job and moved to the Big Apple to try my luck. Needless to say, it was easier said than done. I found an apartment, got a portfolio, and went searching for an agent. To support myself, I got a job as a bartender. The tips you can make bartending are unbelievable. All you have to do is smile, look good, and talk. Believe it or not, I would recommend bartending for college grads coming out of school without a job. Trust me: you will make money.

I did the bartending gig for a while, got bored, and applied for a job as a personal trainer at a gym—another idea of one of my girlfriends. Besides, as a model you have to stay in good shape. So I was able to work out free, train people, and make money. Soon modeling gigs starting coming in. This was fun, but I didn't make the kind of money I thought I would be making. I guess if I been more committed and beat the pavement more, I would have gotten more gigs. My heart wasn't into it. After two years, I gave it up and moved to Minnesota to be with my girlfriend and we eventually got married. I went back into the insurance business.

I was living the regular middle-class life. Going to work and returning home to be with my wife. One day at work, while at lunch, I heard an airplane fly over and I thought, *that's what I want to do*. I called my wife at work and mentioned it to her. She said, so why don't you do it? Be a pilot. You only live once, she told me. By now the Internet was up and running. My wife Googled the requirements and found out corrected 20/20 vision was acceptable for commercial pilots. Within a month's time, I tendered my letter of resignation, and enrolled in flight school in Florida.

Normally it takes twelve months to get a license. I got mine in seven and would have gotten it in six, but I took off a month to welcome the birth of my first son. I can't express how happy I was to be a licensed pilot and welcome my son all in a year's time. Man, I was on top of the world with a son, a great wife, and my dream job of becoming a pilot.

With the license under by belt, I then had to get six hundred flight-time hours to be eligible to fly a commercial plane. That wasn't an easy task. Getting a license to fly is not cheap and getting flight hours isn't any cheaper. Unless you own your own airplane, you have to pay a licensed pilot to fly with you or take additional classes to get flying hours. I signed on with the Civil Air Patrol, a nonprofit organization that performs search and rescue operations. This helped me get closer to the six hundred hours needed. Once I got my hours, I started looking for pilot jobs—another challenging task. You just don't see ads in the classified section of the paper looking for pilots, but I didn't let that stop me. To fill my time while looking for work as a pilot, I started my own business, Errands Express, which basically ran errands for people. I had the business for just over a year before I got hired on by a regional airline. At that point, I closed the business, and, as they say the rest is history.

It took me some time to eventually get to where I wanted to be in life, but I got there and had fun along the way. You have to have fun and enjoy what you are doing. Never give up. Even when it looks like your dreams are far away, keep going after them. There were many times I felt that I wasn't getting any closer to where I wanted to be. As you can see, I had a number of jobs before I got my dream job, and to be honest those jobs weren't for me. I'm just glad I realized it before the jobs did, if you know what I mean.

Now my life is complete. I have a wonderful family. A beautiful wife, two sons, and a great job that I had always wanted. I can't ask for anything else. Well, I wouldn't mind winning the lottery so that I could buy my own airplane. That's my next passion. Stay tuned.

∽

CHAPTER 29

Don't Stop Thinking About Tomorrow

Tyrone's Story
Entrepreneur/ Business Owner
The Barber Extraordinaire

I couldn't give my future and that of my family to a company and say you know what's best manage it. Why should I feel comfortable letting a corporation decide my future? How do I know the company will do what is best for me? The way I see it companies today are looking out for themselves and individuals should do the same. Look out for yourself and manage your own future the best way you can. I know this first hand.

I worked for International Paper Company for eight years and made good money. I was a top performer at IP and had the respect of my supervisors and colleagues. I was the 'go to guy' when things needed to get done. I felt good having a job that I knew extremely well and enjoyed. I was providing for my family, had two cars, a place to stay and was happy.

My perfect world started to change when my schedule at work changed. I found myself spending more time at work and less time with my family and no time for outside activities. I became moody. My relationship with my colleagues became tense. I was a bit irritable at home (around my wife and two sons). I knew I had to make a change, but I didn't know what kind of change. Leaving IP wasn't an option, for it was my families livelihood. As time went on it became evident, I had to leave IP but I didn't know how. One day at work a colleague (a guardian angel) heard me complaining about my new schedule and having to work the night shift. He walked up to me and whispered in my ear, "A barber never has to work nightshifts." I looked at him and thought he can't be serious. Cutting hair was something I did on the side for family and a few friends (including him). I never thought of being a barber full time let alone making it a profession and this guy didn't know anything about my financial situation. International Paper Company was my life, and I was making good money.

As I started taking stock of my life, what I wanted to do and where I wanted to go, I knew what I had to do. My choices were stay at IP and be miserable at work and irritable at home or believe in myself and do something about it. I talked to my wife and we made the decision, I would become my own boss. Now I don't want this to sound as though I _ we (my wife) just made the decision on the fly. We thought long and hard and prayed about my new future and career move which would have major consequences on our family, if I failed.

With just a little money, I resigned from IP and entered barber school. I had a part-time job as a chemical dependency counselor at the local hospital. I was able to use the money from that to help pay the bills. Within nine months, I got my barber's license. My first official clients were my clients at the hospital. Slowly, word got out that I was a licensed barber and my business started to grow. I have to admit I did wonder if I would be able support my family cutting hair and working part-time as a counselor. My wife, Semeka, is my biggest supporter and she saw the potential. She knew that I could run my own business and make it work. As my business grew, eventually I had to leave my job as a counselor.

I couldn't be any happier today. Leaving IP is one of the best things I've done. My barber business has grown and is still growing. I took a big gamble when I left IP and so far it's a gamble that worked. Everybody has to decide what works for them and do it. What worked for me probably wouldn't necessarily worked for the next person. But I will say be cautious on counting on a company or a job you don't own to chart your future. Putting all your eggs in one basket will hurt if the company decides to close or let you go. Unfortunately, most companies only have their best interests in mind and not necessarily yours.

Shortly after I resigned from IP it closed. Not that I had anything to do with it, but the company realized that their market producing paper was drying up. They had a different business plan. I was blessed to have left when I did. I often think about my colleagues and other workers who had their future in IP.

You have to always look ahead and don't stop thinking about tomorrow or the next day. You never know what will happen. You have to be a head of the curve. Sure my barber business could dry up, but people will always need a haircut. A barber is one of those recession proof professions just like a mortician.

I am now looking to buy the building my shop is in and becoming a landlord.

༺༻

CHAPTER 30

Opportunities

Opportunities can come in different ways. One is through self-realization. What do you really want to do? What will your next steps be? Are you going to follow your passion and look for another job? Go back to school? Become a teacher? Stay in the field of finance or medicine? There is a world of opportunity out there waiting for you. Choose one and start living. All you have to do is breathe and go for it. Don't be afraid. It might take time for you to get to where you want to go, but just believe and know that you will and can do it. No matter what the sacrifice, just do it!

If you are reading this and you never thought you would be without a job and have no savings squirreled away, don't be disheartened. File for unemployment, register with your nearest temp agency, and agree to do administrative work or whatever is available. Don't turn your back on working at a hotel, department store, or any skilled jobs (plumbers and electricians can make a lot and the field isn't saturated). Working at a restaurant or being a bartender are two other jobs you might want to consider. You can make a lot in tips. No, these jobs aren't by any means a fall from grace or a step backward in your career—it's money that will keep you afloat and out of a bad relationship (bad job) until the next best thing comes your way. Think positive, redirect your energies, and make it happen! Even in the worst economy you can reinvent yourself and create a job. Just don't give up or give in to self-pity.

Finally and unfortunately, you can always climb back into bed with the same job relationship (look for the same job you previously had that you didn't like). The results will be the same. One day you will wake up to the sound of the job saying *it just isn't into you.*

❧

CHAPTER 31

Rules of the Road

Below are a few bullet points to keep in mind when you are on a job. You should also use these points if and when you find out *That Job Just Isn't Into You!*

- Always have a backup plan
- Don't panic
- See it coming
- Maintain composure
- Never let them see you sweat
- Everything is transient; nothing lasts forever
- Cradle to grave no longer exists with a job
- Losing a job is not an embarrassment
- Do a postmortem to identify lessons learned
- Mourn for a day
- Accept that it is over
- Rediscover yourself
- Cut out a new path
- Find your passion
- Take control of your career

- Be flexible in your search for another job
- Cast your job fishing net wider and in different waters
- Don't wrap your identity in a job
- Don't let the job define you—you define the job
- Each job is a stepping-stone
- Network outside of your industry
- Tailor your résumé for each opportunity
- Never give up
- Budget finances
- Keep six months' living expenses in reserve

෨෧

CHAPTER 32

You're Taking It Personal

Wait one frickin' minute! It was personal. They all had it in for me and that's why I lost my job.

If you can't accept *That Job Just Isn't Into You!* after reading this entire book, go ahead and have your psycho meltdown.

Just be sure to give this book a mention in your viral video posting on YouTube.

‿

NOTES

Acknowledgments

First, I would like to thank my family, friends and associates who allowed me to share their stories with readers. Your stories and advice on survival and reinvention is one of the reasons I wrote this book. Hopefully, your experiences that can be painful, embarrassing and stressful will help to remove the stigma of being fired, laid off, terminated or whatever fancy term your boss chooses to call it. Because at the end of the day it could be *"That Job Just Isn't Into You!"*

Special thanks to the following: June Weinstein, who suggested I create a job opportunity for myself; Raymond Hinton, my accountant, who believed in the book's concept; Terri Sohrab, a financial guru, friend and mentor, who believes in everything I do. I can hear Terri now saying: "Just do it Baby." To my high school librarian, Mrs. Harriett Washington, thank you for stepping in and giving this book your early morning review. You are a life saver. I cannot forget to think Linda, my creative friend. We spent a lot hours brainstorming on ideas. Your apartment is an ideal writer's den. We still have to finish up the million or so open items on the schedule. Where do we start? I can't leave out my creative team at CreateSpace (Abdur, Kim, Molly, Maria, Emily and Kristen) thank you all. Finally, to my Mom or Ma. Thank you for all the love and nurturing which gave me a solid foundation to be committed to a

job. Also thank you, for keeping the first piece I ever wrote to my
third grade teacher, Mrs. Dorothy Wardell titled "Keep away."
I love you dearly, Ma.

෮෨

About The Author

Rob Harper is a seasoned executive with over sixteen years of combined experience in the banking and journalism fields. He began his financial career as a consultant with Citi Private Bank where he held various managerial positions and was involved in the decision-making process of hiring and laying off staff. Prior to entering the financial sector Harper was as a journalist for a major daily newspaper in northwest Arkansas. He has had articles featured on The Huffington Post, where he is a frequent blogger on employment and politics, CNN and CNNireport. Harper resides in New York City.

༄

www.ingramcontent.com/pod-product-compliance
Lightning Source LLC
Chambersburg PA
CBHW051546170526
45165CB00002B/897